Rule Y

Reduce Your Stress, Regain Your Control & Restore Your Calm

by

Cassie Farren

To Paula,

Anything is possible when you

Rule Your World,

love

Cassie

X

Published in 2017 by Welford Publishing

Copyright © Cassie Farren 2017

ISBN: Paperback 978-0-9931296-5-0

ISBN: ebook 978-0-9931296-4-3

A catalogue record for this book is available from the British Library.

Disclaimer

This book contains general reference information and is not intended as a substitute for consulting with a medical practitioner. If you suspect you have a medical problem please always speak to a health professional.

Dedication

For Kieron & Lennie

Acknowledgements

Thank you to Michelle Emerson from Painless Online Publishing for editing my book and for being such a great support through this process.

Thank you to Kim Macleod from Indie Authors World for designing my beautiful book cover.

Thank you to my mum, dad and sister for always believing in me.

Contents

Rule Your World..1

Rule 1 - Give yourself a break 9

Rule 2 - Find a way or find an excuse.......................14

Rule 3 - Embrace the power of the "F" word! 24

Rule 4 - The little things are the big things...............39

Rule 5 - Embrace the power of the "M" word! 60

Rule 6 - It's okay not to be okay 73

Rule 7 - Don't stop now!..87

"The Rules" - A Summary 91

Resources 95

About the Author 96

Contact Cassie..97

Cassie's First Book 98

Rule Your World

Let's break the ice first, shall we?

It's not easy.

Day in, day out, tirelessly fighting that relentless battle in your head. You have done your best to carry on with your life whilst keeping a smile plastered on your face. The exhaustion from pretending to be stronger than you feel is kicking in. You are becoming more and more drained from the emotional rollercoaster that has become your normality.

From the outside looking in your life looks good. No one knows that your head is constantly spinning. No one understands that you feel trapped inside an invisible prison. No one can hear that negative voice that follows you everywhere and refuses to shut up.

It's not easy.

You have *always* lived your life with such pride and determination. You are a strong, capable person who hates feeling out of control. You feel like you should know better. You feel like you should be able to cope. You feel like you should be able to hold everything together, just like you've always done.

1

You may not be sure how your life got to this point but you do know it has been going on for too long. You have started to overthink everything, you have stopped trusting your own judgement and you miss the carefree person you used to be. It shouldn't be this way, should it? All you want is to get this mess out of your head, and ultimately your life, but where do you start?

You may be wondering if this is the part where I declare how wonderful my life is, and promise to make your life the same, before 'impressing' you with my amazing expert status! Let me see what I can do.

Dear hopeful reader,

Please find below my wonderful credentials;

Career: my last full-time job was as a mortgage advisor. I studied extremely hard to gain my professional qualifications whilst working full-time and bringing up my eldest son on my own. When the relentless pressure caused me to wake up every night in tears I knew I had a decision to make. My health or my career? I felt like a complete failure as I handed in my notice with no job to go to. I had become a shadow of the woman I used to be. So much so that when I drove into the car park for my next job interview, I almost didn't go in. Why? Because I didn't feel good enough. The role I was being interviewed for was a hotel cleaner (in case you were wondering cleaner wasn't a typo!). I was so relieved to get the job. Yes, it was drastic but I had to do something to rescue my head from the mess it had become. I continued to work at the hotel for 5 years before being made redundant, as my part-time hours didn't fit in with their new restructure.

In 2013, (2 years after leaving the hotel and after dipping my toes into the waters of network marketing) I set up my own business. I should have felt so proud of myself for launching with nothing more than hope, determination and a Facebook page. Instead I went to bed and cried, scared that people would laugh at me or judge me. I had no experience of setting up a business, no relevant qualifications and no money. If I had known how hard the last four years were going to be there is no way I would have started. Financially and emotionally there have been so many challenges that have literally knocked me off my feet, time and time again.

Personal life: this has been a combination of highs, lows, and Jeremy Kyle moments! I became a single mum for the third time last year (in case you were wondering third also wasn't a typo, either!). It was during this time of chaos and turmoil that I decided enough was enough, I was done. I was done with not valuing myself, I was done with treading over the eggshells in my head and I was done with living a life where I didn't felt good enough.

Believe me, if I could go back in time and give myself a good talking to I would! Hindsight is a wonderful thing. It is easy to blame other people or circumstances for the perceived mistakes you have made. It is easy to live your life as a victim who carries the burden of hurt, resentment and anger.

It is *not* easy to take responsibility for your perceived mistakes and commit to doing whatever it takes to move forward with your life. I have made a commitment that I will not allow the ghosts from my past to steal my future happiness. I owe it to myself and I owe it to my amazing children Kieron and Lennie.

Current status: I would love to tell you that everything has gone from strength to strength and that we all lived happily ever after, but that wouldn't be the truth. Despite finding some deeply hidden strength and resilience it has been the hardest year of my life.

I don't consider myself to be a resident in the land of 'Fake Believe' where the unspoken law requires sharing every hour of your rose-tinted life, accompanied by the hashtag #soblessedsohappysodeluded (spot the odd one out!).

Joking aside, against all the odds, I had got to a place where I felt very positive and I was proud of how I had progressed. I had been working consistently on having a clear head and was convinced that *this* was my time. I

4

was ready to test my wings and fly high. My past was firmly in the past and n*othing* was going to come between me and my final destination of inspiring a new generation of empowerment.

Life had other plans, only one week before I began writing this book I could feel myself sliding into a 'dark dip'. Thankfully I managed to use the tools I will be sharing with you and got myself out and back on track after three days. This may not seem like a big deal but if you've ever slipped into a 'dark dip' you will know that every hour can feel like a day and every day can feel like a week. You also don't know whilst experiencing it, when it will end.

I don't know where these horrible feelings came from. I couldn't blame them on having the 'hangover blues' as I rarely drink alcohol, let alone in excess (well, there was a night out in December when I rolled in at 3am, lost my phone and was ill for the next 2 days, but this was an extremely rare event – never to be repeated!). But now we have that confession out in the open can we put it to one side and forget about it? Because I have!

Anyway, I digress. There was definitely no post-alcohol blues, just a dark cloud that followed me everywhere I went day and night. I felt lonely. I have a close circle of friends but I didn't want to see or speak to anybody. I could have gone out but I had no desire to leave the house. I carried on being Cassie the mum, Cassie the business owner and Cassie the daughter, whilst pretending to the outside world that Cassie was 'fine, thank you' if anyone asked.

I could feel myself sinking lower but at the same time I was trying to fight it and felt so angry with myself. My negative voice was shouting, "You are such an idiot, Cassie, you need to sort yourself out, and get a grip!" I felt like a fool and life felt like hard work. I was finding it hard to see the positive in anything, let alone writing a book about it!

My negative voice is even whispering to me now, "Do you really think anyone wants to read your book, who do you think you are to call yourself an expert?" You'll be pleased to know I have told it to shut up. Nothing will stop me from publishing this book even whilst my life could be considered a beautiful mess.

I don't believe there is a permanent solution for sorting out your head once and for all, or for living an unrealistic perfectly positive life. What I do believe is that you have the power to drastically reduce the frequency and the severity of your 'dark dips'. I am living proof that you can be the one who controls your head and ultimately your life, but only if you *want* to change.

It's not easy.

But it is simple.

If you are half-heartedly here just looking for someone else to inspire you and do the work for you, then you are wasting your time. You may, however, enjoy reading my first book which has already inspired many people and received more than 50 five-star reviews, *The Girl Who Refused to Quit* ☺

This is the link to my first book if you'd like to check it out **http://amzn.to/2uo4to5**

Are you still here?

Good. I've got a few quick questions to check we are on the same page – literally!

Are you ready to feel:

- More productive?
- More positive?
- More focused?
- More confident?
- More energised?
- More relaxed?

Would you like to:

Reduce your stress, Regain Your Control & Restore Your calm so that you too can

Rule Your World?

Excellent.

Now that I know you are serious about creating positive changes that will lead to stress-free living, and you know that I am ~~not normal~~ a 'unique' author, I would officially like to welcome you to my book.

From the hopeful author,

Cassie

P.S Connect with me on Twitter @cassiefarren1 and share your progress through the book using #RuleYourWorld

P.P.S Come and connect with me in the FREE "Rule Your World" Facebook group for support and inspiration. www.facebook.com/groups/ruleyourworldtribe

Rule 1 - Give yourself a break

If you're honest with yourself something hasn't felt right for a while, has it? Every day is beginning to blend into the next and life feels more mundane than meaningful. The negative voice in your head is always shouting at you, yet the voice that comes out of your mouth, when asked, says "I'm good thanks". Let's be honest, can you remember how it feels to really switch off, relax and unwind? You know that you need to have some time out but can you realistically get through the day or relax and switch off without a strong coffee (or glass of wine!) in your hand?

I want you to know that you are not a failure, you are not weak and you certainly are not alone.

No one is invincible, you are human and there comes a point where you need to take stock and admit that everything is not 'ok'. And it's fine to do that. If you are ready to finally put an end to the silent epidemic that is spreading in your mind then you are in the right place.

Looking for guidance is not a sign of weakness. You are here for a reason, and making the decision that you want to create change is definitely a sign of strength.

Why did this happen?

Think of your mind like a brand-new computer. You entered this world as a beautiful bundle of pure innocence with a blank memory ready to be programmed. You were perfect in every way and lived a carefree and unapologetic life where all of your needs were immediately met.

As you grew older you quickly evolved, learning from the important people in your life and the experiences you encountered. This came from your parents, siblings, friends, teachers, partners and jobs, to name a few. Unfortunately, not all of your 'programming' experiences are positive. As a result, you acquired and installed invisible layers. These layers began to form your habits and beliefs - some positive but more often than not they were negative. You may have been told that 'you were shy' by a teacher or that 'you would never succeed' by an old boss or that you were 'an embarrassment' by an ex-partner. You repeated these beliefs until you came to accept that this is who you are.

You have been programmed, shaped and moulded throughout your life by many different people, sometimes without you knowing. Some may have left small imprints, others, deeper scars. Without realising it you may have been conforming to many values and beliefs that are not truly yours. If you aren't living your life in accordance with your own values and beliefs this is when you can begin to feel lost and that something doesn't feel right.

There's more, too!

On top of these layers it is said that an average adult has 50,000 thoughts per day. Out of those 50,000 it is said that 70% of those are negative and that we repeat the majority of these thoughts day in, day out.

And more!

On top of those thoughts we absorb the negative influence of the news and media. We also have the constant newsfeed (aka dramafeed) on social media, we also have some friends, (and sometimes family) who love a good old moan and whinge about absolutely anything and everything.

You have been everything to everyone for as long as you can remember and in the process, you've neglected the most important person in your life, you! Right now, you may not feel very important but if you start to make yourself a priority you will be amazed at how quickly this change will ripple into every area of your life.

Give yourself a break!

I want you to know that you have a choice. You can carry on as you are, blaming old beliefs and emotional scars for the way you are. You can pick away at them so that any damage feels justified or you can decide right here and right now that you are ready to heal the old scars, and ready to move on.

The good news is that just like your mind can be programmed with negative influences it can also be wiped clean and reprogrammed with positivity. Once you start to unveil these layers, you will feel increasingly calm and that negative voice in your head will stop shouting at you. Your confidence and respect for yourself will increase and your relationships will see a positive impact too as you begin to live a more relaxed and carefree life where you are in control.

I am well aware that when you are already feeling overwhelmed the last thing you need is endless information and theories. I have kept this book short in length and in bite sized chunks so that it feels achievable to finish what you have started.

You may like to have a notebook to hand as you continue to read "The Rules."

I know you can do this.

Rule 1: Give yourself a break.

The overwhelm in your head is not your fault. It has built up due to an accumulation of 'life layers' which have built up over many years.

These layers have joined forces with the added pressure of work, family and financial pressure with extra added pressure from social media and the busyness of everyday life.

Draw a line under what's been and gone. Your past can't be changed, but from now on you can commit to living a calmer life where you are in control.

Make the decision now to stop emotionally beating yourself up and decide that you are ready to incorporate stress-free living into your life.

Rule 2 - Find a way or find an excuse

Excuse = the lie you tell yourself to make yourself feel better about justifying your lack of responsibility for your own life.

Ouch! Writing that was a bit uncomfortable but I have to be honest with you, and in order for you to create a positive change, I need you to be honest with yourself.

Making a positive lasting change is not easy.

Have you ever committed to making a change in your life and it hasn't worked? This can leave you feeling deflated and in a less motivated state than before you started. You give up on the idea, give up on yourself and then find an excuse to justify why your plan didn't work.

Social comparison.

On top of feeling deflated it is so easy to feel like everyone else in the world is living a perfect life, mainly thanks to social media where at any time, day or night, you can see the filtered highlights of someone else's life.

This is not real life!

How have we got to the point where we are led to believe that it is normal to wake up in a full face of make-up, hair perfectly curled as the beautiful morning sunlight streams through the window, whilst drinking a cappuccino with hand crafted chocolate sprinkles in the shape of a unicorn?! Ok, I may have over-exaggerated slightly with the unicorn thing, but seriously, #getalife!

Believe it or not I am a big fan of social media. It has played a huge part in my business and I love the power of it when used in a positive way. What infuriates me is when people seem to care more about their online life than they do their real life. It's easy to think that everyone else's life is perfect, especially if you are feeling overwhelmed with yours, and this can make it harder to find that initial confidence to even get started on your goals.

Top Tip #1 You do not have to scroll through your social media newsfeed!

There is a good change that a large percent of your newsfeed will be negative. You may think, 'Oh it's just another friend having another rant' but all this pessimism adds to your already overwhelmed head, which will make it even harder for you to break free and make a positive change. You can use social media in a positive way by joining like-minded groups, or use it to message friends individually.

Top Tip #2 Keep it real!

Just because you have seen all your friends perfectly filtered 'best bits' on social media does not mean that you or your life is not up to scratch. Even if you have been inspired by someone else's journey on social media whether it's through weight loss or growing their business, remember to never compare someone else's middle to your beginning. This is your journey, so start where you are.

Who ate all the (mince) pies?

I'm going to go slightly off on a tangent here so bear with me.

The best example that most of us can relate to when it comes to making a positive change (and the challenges it brings) is the post-Christmas resolutions to live a healthier lifestyle and lose weight – something the majority of the country does every New Year.

Now, before you all start shouting, "What would you know about this Cassie, you aren't overweight so how you would have any idea of how hard this can be?" I need to tell you something. When I was pregnant with my boys I put on three stone in each pregnancy and found it hard to lose the weight.

When I split up with Kieron's dad I drastically lost a lot of weight through 'the stress and self- destruct diet'. NB, I do not recommend this! I hated myself and got into a pattern of hardly eating and then getting so hungry that I would binge eat, and then hate myself and go back to hardly eating. I was in a very low place. Even though I weighed less than eight stone I was still convinced I was fat, ugly and worthless. I became obsessed with my scales and I was miserable.

Thankfully, over time, I found the strength to rebuild my body confidence from the inside out and I learned how to accept myself. I threw out my scales over 13 years ago and I now very rarely weigh myself. So, you're right, I'm not overweight but I do understand how hard it can be to make a positive lasting change, especially if you're feeling overwhelmed right now.

Let's get back to those mince pies (and anything else that can be purchased in the Christmas aisle!). You have decided that the 'new you' will emerge as soon as all of this food has been eaten. You join the gym, sign up to all the classes, buy a whole new wardrobe of gym clothes, buy a state of the art smoothie maker and some wheatgrass supplements thrown in for good measure.

Once the New Year's Eve hangover has disappeared and you have vowed never to drink again, you decide that nothing is going to come between you and your healthy new lifestyle. You start off really keen but after a few weeks, life starts to get in the way and the visits to the gym become less frequent. You haven't seen the results you were hoping for despite 'being good'. Feeling disheartened you console yourself with a takeaway and a bottle of wine and tell yourself that your life is too busy to go to the gym.

Sound familiar?

When I worked in the hotel spa I would see this scenario all the time. There would be an influx of new members joining the gym with bags of enthusiasm. Then you'd see them a few weeks later relaxing in the spa lounge with a cappuccino and a chocolate bar, moaning that they weren't seeing a difference in their weight.

I have made this scenario light-hearted as I feel it's a very relatable situation but the demoralising side effects are very real. Most people find they stay stuck in denial for a while as they continue to self-sabotage and then when it gets too much they begin the cycle again, and convince themselves, 'This is it! This time I will really do it! I will achieve my goal'. The cycle resumes, full of hope, but if the overwhelm increases it's all too easy to fall off the wagon and once again turn to a chocolate bar or a few glasses of wine for comfort.

In summary, making a change can feel hard but making a lasting change can feel impossible!

I believe you will never make any positive, lasting change in your life until you clear some space in your head. Whether that's losing weight or taking control of those self-sabotaging thoughts, you have to sort your head out first.

You are swimming upstream.

It's like you are trying to swim upstream, against the current, in thick treacle! Just as you are making progress there is a huge storm that washes you back down to where you started from and you have to find the strength to start again.

Why is it so damn hard to make a change?

As I shared with you in chapter 1, you have approximately 50,000 thoughts a day. That's 1,8250,000 thoughts per year. The majority of these thoughts are worrying, fearful or overthinking problems. If you do a quick calculation of 1,8250,000 x how many years you have been alive, that is a lot of negative thoughts!

There is no magic wand for willpower!

Unfortunately, you can't buy willpower; if anyone invented that they would be a billionaire! But don't give up hope. I will be sharing with you in chapter 5 what I believe is the secret weapon for lasting willpower. Until then I want you think about your 'why'.

How can you stop the excuses and find a way?

If you want to find a way you have to find your 'why'.

To make a positive lasting change you have to know why you want to change and this has to have meaning for you.

Finding your why creates an emotional attachment to your goals. This is a fundamental part of your success. You will learn to let go of any excuses and find a way to create a lasting change in your life.

Find your 'why' exercise:

To find your 'why' answer question 1 and keep on asking yourself "why?" until you reach an answer that has a meaningful connection to you; you may want to write your answers down.

I am going to use an example of a 45-year-old father who is a partner in a law firm and is currently working very long hours.

Question 1: Why do you want to decrease your stress levels and feel calmer? (There is no right or wrong answer)

Example answer: I want to feel calmer and decrease my stress levels so that I don't feel so angry all the time.

Q: Why?

Example answer: I don't like the person I have become.

Q: Why?

Example answer: I don't like the person I have become as I am snappy all the time. I feel bad that I don't spend enough quality time with my family.

Q: Why?

I want to have a positive relationship with my family and have a calmer atmosphere in our house.

Q: Why?

I want to be a positive role model to my children and want them to know that they can always speak to me if they are upset or have any problems at school.

Q: Why?

I was bullied at school which really knocked my confidence. I never want my children to experience feeling so alone and afraid as I did.

There is his "why"!

It is very powerful and may initially seem unrelated to the initial question but this is where the power lies to making a positive lasing change.

It's your turn.

Go through the questions and find out why it is important for you reduce your stress levels, regain your control and to feel calmer. Go with your gut instinct and keep on asking yourself why, until you get to a reason that is meaningful to you. It may help to write this down so you have a reminder to come back to if things don't go to plan.

There may be times when you feel like you are taking one step forward and two steps back, and that's ok, the way to get back on track quickly is to go back and remember your why.

There may be times when you self-diagnose yourself with P.O.M Syndrome (Poor Old Me!) and that's also ok, you are human. We all have those moments of 'It wasn't me, it was my past!' That's ok, too, as this is what you have always done, this is your default. Slipping back into victim mode removes all of your control which, in turn, defeats the object. You have to take responsibility for your actions to move forward and create a positive lasting change.

Rule 2: Find a way or find an excuse.

Creating a positive lasting change in your life begins with finding your 'why'.

You know the importance of letting go of your old excuses and P.O.M syndrome. Finding your 'why' will

22

help you to keep your motivation, even when challenges occur.

Excuses are just words that you use to justify not being responsible. If you give away the power of your responsibility then you are not in control. If you are not in control you will never be able to make a positive lasting change in your head or your life.

Rule 3 - Embrace the power of the "F" word!

I'm going to be brave, put on my big girl pants and talk about the forbidden "F" word – no, not that one!

Feelings!

There you go, I've said it out loud. Feelings! Feelings! Feelings!

Let's talk about feelings. They can either be your best friend or your worst enemy. They can take control of your moods, determine your actions, and if you're not careful they can take control of your entire life. They don't (but perhaps should?) come with a bright red flashing warning light to give you prior notice they are about to change. Feelings can transform (sometimes in milliseconds) from good to bad or from happy to sad. They can also erase any sense of normal logic – and how infuriating is that?

You only have to read my last paragraph to see why so many people choose the easy option and avoid the dreaded "F" word altogether.

And I get it.

24

After all, we are strong, independent human beings who like to feel that we are firmly in control of our lives. If we do choose to express our emotions we enlist the expert help of our smart phone, and a wide variety of helpful yellow emojis ☺! The last thing we want to do is admit to ourselves, let alone anyone else, that we are not coping, or show any signs of vulnerability or weakness.

Much as we love to hate our feelings, acknowledging them is an integral part of creating the lasting change we want to see in our lives. I am breaking the mould, here, by committing to sharing a whole chapter on feelings, as I truly believe that once you can see them in a different light you too will realise just how powerful they can be, especially when they are on your side.

You may be thinking, 'Hmmm… you've not convinced me yet, Cassie' and that's ok. I promise I won't go all happy clappy on you or ask you to do any weird woo woo stuff! All I ask is that you read on with an open mind. And if you're the type of person who prefers cold, hard evidence, you must keep reading because I'm sharing some very interesting scientific proof later in the chapter.

Shall we continue?

Deep breath… here we go!

Why do feelings exist?

The most popular theory is that our feelings exist to help us survive. Going back to our cavemen days, if there was a threat from a predator when we were out hunting, the feeling of fear would create a rush of blood to our limbs along with the rush of adrenaline to our brain so we could quickly run back to the safety of our cave. So in the very early days of our evolution, our feelings were there to help us to literally stay alive. But, thankfully, things have changed. We no longer have the threat of predators chasing us when we are out looking for food. Ok, so occasionally, we might bump into angry people in the supermarket (especially in December!) but they are unlikely to threaten our safety. Well, unless you grab the last box of Quality Street on Christmas Eve!

Why don't we talk about our feelings?

When positive feelings are working for you they can be used in a good way to form, develop and strengthen relationships. When negative feelings are working against you they can quickly spiral out of control, leaving you unsure and worried. There is often no logical explanation behind these feelings which means that sometimes they don't make sense, even to us. Even if you can find the courage to explain how you are feeling it can be hard for others to understand. They may try to reassure you that 'no one else worries about that', and I'm sure they have your best interests at heart. Their intention is to genuinely try to help you find a logical solution to ease your worry.

26

They, no doubt, will want to help stop these thoughts from spinning around your head, but hearing a logical explanation isn't going to help.

The reason for this is that the negative thought you are experiencing isn't logical, so a logical answer isn't going to counteract this or make it go away. Their best intentions can sometimes leave you feeling even more alone and misunderstood as the worry continues.

Hiding your feelings

Suppressing emotions is a coping strategy many people use. This can be down to low self-esteem, if you don't feel worthy of expressing your feelings. You may feel that even if you do share them, nothing will change so what's the point? Pretending they don't exist or increasing your alcohol consumption to numb them won't work either - I have researched both in the past! The emotions will get deeper and your negative feelings will escalate – leaving you feeling even more isolated, alone and worried.

"Men and women who avoid emotions, especially negative ones, are more likely to experience high anxiety in their lifetime."

This is quoted from an article on www.mysahana.org, 'Emotion Suppression: Effects on mental and physical health'.

It doesn't help that in our society we have become conditioned to think and feel in a certain way. Growing up, we are told that 'children should be seen and not heard'. As adults we are also led to believe that expressing our feelings is a sign of weakness. No matter what happens, living in England we have a very stiff upper lip way of coping. We keep calm and carry on regardless (after a nice cup of tea, of course!).

It's not just in your head!

We can also experience physical symptoms from negative thoughts. It is known that the hormone, adrenaline, is triggered by stress and anxiety.

I found this explanation from www.anxietyguru.net where he explains what happens in our body;

"Once your brain receives a message that you are in trouble, adrenaline is pumped into your bloodstream and causes your heart rate to increase (increased oxygen) dilates pupils for better vision) increases sweat production (keeps you cool in case you need to run) suppresses immune system (not needed in danger situations) and creates a general (but awful) feeling of fear.

This reaction is supposed to help you survive a potentially life-threatening situation, but 99% of the time your reaction is a false alarm and even though you feel like you are ready for action, there is nothing going on."

Or is there?

As we go through life it is inevitable that at some point we will face fear, uncertainty and worry. This could be triggered by many situations in your life, such as a marriage breakdown, or an impending redundancy.

*Your body still experiences the same feeling of fear as the caveman did but it does not know that you are no longer a caveman/cavewoman.

*Your body also has no way to tell that this is an emotional threat you are dealing with, not a physical one.

*Your body will still trigger the same rush of adrenaline to your brain and at the same time a rush of blood moves away from your brain.

*Your body has successfully prepared you for fight or flight mode but it is unaware you will not be using this adrenaline in your mind, or the blood in your limbs, to run back to your cave.

There is literally nowhere for the adrenaline to go, and with less blood in our brain it makes it even harder to think logically, especially if you have to deal with the added physical symptoms on top of the worry and fear.

29

It's no wonder that these negative thoughts can spiral out of control quickly when the emotional threat and physical symptoms combine.

How can you quickly stop this negative spiral and take back control of your thoughts?

Here comes the science part!

Chris Walton MSc, has written an amazing book called *The Gamma Mindset* published in 2012. The extract that I will be sharing below quite literally blew my mind.

Your heart is the key

"Most of us think of the heart as a pump that propels blood around the body. This is true, but researchers at the leading edge of science are telling us it is so much more than a mere pump. The trouble is, this information is not widely known.

Traditionally we think of the brain as the central computer of the body. It receives information from the five physical senses and sends information signals to the body to produce the desired actions and to drive physiological functions. I suspect that few of you know that your heart is an organ that can learn, remember, feel and sense independently of your brain! It's true! In fact the research that has shown the heart to be a sensory organ led to the new medical discipline called

30

neurocardiology, which is the study of the connections and communication between the nervous system and the heart.

Because the coherence of your heart-brain connection is so important to the science of how we repattern our subconscious minds with new empowering beliefs, here is an overview of the four ways the heart communicates with the brain, according to research from the discipline of neurocardiology and other areas, such as the work of the Heart Math Institute.

1) *The first route of heart-brain communication is the most obvious; through the transmission of nerve impulses via the nervous system.*

2) *The second way is with chemicals such as hormones and neurotransmitters. It was a huge surprise to researchers to find the heart producing and using biochemicals that they previously thought only the brain used. The heart produces such powerful hormones as atrial peptide, which reduces the stress hormone, cortisol. That the heart actually produces this peptide means that, contrary to previous biological knowledge, the heart - and not just the brain - is designed to help relieve stress. The heart also produces oxytocin, which is known as the 'love hormone'. Isn't it interesting that the organ we associate so closely with love actually produces the love hormone? The heart also produces dopamine. Dopamine is produced for many reasons, one of which is to facilitate*

learning, especially when we are forming new habits and
behaviours.

3) The third way the heart communicates with the brain is
    bio-physically - that is, through energy fields that affect
    the body. For example, when the heart beats, it creates a
    wave of energy called a blood pressure wave. This blood
    pressure wave reaches the brain before the blood and
    changes brain activity. As the blood pressure wave
    changes, so does the electrical activity of the brain.

4) The fourth way, and possibly the most exciting way, is via
    purely energetic connections, such as electromagnetic
    fields. The heart is our main electrical power centre. It
    produces 2½ watts of electrical power, which is 40 to 60
    times more wattage than is produced by the electrical
    activity of the brain. Interestingly, you can record your
    heartbeat anywhere on your body. That's because every
    time your heart beats, the electrical field it produces
    permeates every cell, forming a potential body-wide
    communication network. In fact your thoughts and
    feelings are communicated to every cell of your body via
    this electromagnetic superhighway. What is more, this
    electromagnetic field doesn't just radiate throughout
    your body, but actually streams from you to the outside
    world, in a 360-degree field that is shaped like a torus (a
    ring doughnut) and that radiates up to 15 feet outside
    your body. It is actually thought to extend much further,
    but our current measuring equipment can only confirm
    its extension to this distance.

From 'The Gamma Mindset' by Chris Walton MSc
www.GammaMindset.com

Back to non-scientific Cassie now. ☺

Chris's book has received some outstanding reviews and endorsements. This is part of the foreword;

"Every part of this book is substantiated by cutting edge science, yet this information is explained with elegance, in an enjoyable and motivating style. I was so impressed with this book that I have made it essential reading for all of my students. The information and techniques transformed me and my life."

- Professor Kazadi Kalangu MD, Brain Surgeon and Vice President of the World Federation of Neurosurgical Societies.

I'd love to know why this powerful information isn't shared in schools, but for now I'm going to get off my soapbox and get back to sharing how you can use the power of your heart to help you live a calmer life where you are in control.

Why is your 'why' so powerful?

The reason I asked you to find your 'why' in chapter 2, and for it to have an emotional connection, is because your heart needs to be on your side to conquer the negative thoughts that can throw you off track when you are trying to achieve your goal. We are creatures of habit and it's not easy to change, but when you can engage your heart and connect your feelings to your goals, that is where the power is.

We are led to believe there is always a logical explanation for everything, including our thoughts.

I beg to differ.

I don't believe a negative thought can be erased or changed with a logical explanation, or that you can be 'talked out of your worry'. This means that the content of the thought (eg whatever you are worrying about) could almost be deemed as irrelevant. This may sound a bit harsh but there is a reason for this, let me explain.

I believe that negative thoughts and worries can be conquered with positive feelings. This is because your heart, the source of your feelings has been proven (in the research documented in Chris Walton's book) to be more powerful than your brain, the source of your thoughts. Therefore, the positive feelings from your heart have the potential to counteract, the negative thoughts from your head.

My real-life case study (NB I had no idea at the time I was being my own case study, I was literally just trying to get through each day!)

34

Last year I booked my first ever appointment with a counsellor. I walked into the office feeling very nervous and apprehensive. Knowing that I was about to pour my entire life out to a stranger was awful. The counsellor went through the standard introduction and asked me why I was there. I replied that I was either coping remarkably well with the chaos in my life, or I was on the verge of having a breakdown. I honestly didn't know which way I was going. After delving into every area of my life and asking many questions about my past I was given this conclusion, "With everything you have been through Cassie, it would be reasonable to expect that it could have taken up to two years to reach a point of acceptance and come to terms with what has happened in your life. You have reached this point in less than six weeks on your own. Our door is always open if you face any more challenges but my advice is not to return for any further sessions as I feel you'd be wasting your money."

Cue me staring at the stranger opposite me in complete silence with my mouth hanging open in complete shock.

Now, before you start thinking I'm boasting about, against all the odds, getting my head out a very big mess in such a short space of time, let me tell you something. I almost didn't include this story in the book. I decided to include it simply because I feel it's important for you to know I haven't always been as calm and in control of my life as I am now. My life had collapsed twice before and I have experienced some spectacular self-destruction. The first time I would guess my head was in a mess for 18 months, the second time about 6 months. This was hidden from the rest of the world, and looking back, perhaps I should have spoken to a counsellor or found help.

When the counsellor asked me what I had done to reach this point so quickly, I had to ask myself that same question, what *had* I done? Without knowing it I had created a "Toolbox for Life" which had empowered me to conquer my negative thoughts with positive feelings.

Despite the many changes in my life that were out of my control, for the first time for as long as I can remember, it felt like I was in control of my head. Until the moment I walked out of the counsellor's office (letting out a huge sigh of relief and shedding a few tears) I had lived in fear of the awful self-destruction creeping up and returning to haunt me. To this day I'm proud to say it hasn't reappeared. I would be lying if I said there hasn't been any dark days, or 'dark dips' but they have been tiny in comparison to the dark months of my past. I am confident that the reason for this is down to me following "The Rules"

If reading this makes you tempted to nickname me Little Miss Positive (!) you may like to know that there have been many times when I wished that my passion and determination would just burn out for good. Believe me, the easy option was not to keep on fighting. As I type these words, I have no idea how my journey will end or how I will get my message out to the world, but I 100% believe in myself and know I will find a way.

I am living proof that "The Rules" really do work!

I will be sharing how to create your own "Toolbox for Life" in Chapter 4. These are my very simple and effective tools to help you feel calmer as you finally take back the control in your head.

It is highly likely that every person you have ever met in your life has experienced unpleasant feelings which have been triggered by negative thoughts. These thoughts have *not* been activated by anything you have done wrong, and you are certainly *not* alone.

"Your power always has been and always will be within you."

– Cassie Farren

Feel free to quote me, tag me and share on social media.

Rule 3: Embrace the power of the "F" word.

We are creatures of habit and it's not easy to change, but when you can engage your heart and connect your feelings to your goals, that is where the power is.

Your feelings have the power to override your negative thoughts. They can literally help you to take back the control in your head and ultimately your life.

Rule 4 - The little things are the big things

Have you ever experienced a thought that started off as a tiny worry and before you realised, it somehow multiplied by 1000, spiralled out of control leaving no space for logic in your head? As I mentioned in chapter 3 you will find that everyone worries about different things, and it's awful when these thoughts spiral out of control. I don't believe there is a way to stop the worry completely. I do believe you can learn to reduce the severity and frequency of your negative thought spirals - aka the 'dark dips' - so that they don't begin to take over your life, but where do you start?

To begin, I'm going to share a very simple, yet powerful tool that I use which will help you recognise and recover quicker from a 'dark dip'. It can also help you to keep your feelings positive which, as you now know, will help to counteract those negative thoughts.

I like to think of all of the guidance I am sharing as tools that you can use at any time and keep in your "Toolbox for Life".

Disclaimer: this is a metaphorical toolbox in case anyone kicks off and complains that they didn't receive their free toolbox with their book! Maybe I could produce some promotional toolboxes to give out as gifts when I have my amazing book launch and silent disco in The Shard?! You'll find out more about my dream world book launch in a few pages time!

Let's get back to adding to your "Toolbox for Life", shall we? A lot of the time we are so busy being busy that we don't give our feelings a second thought. That is until we get to a point where we are feeling down and low, which makes them feel almost impossible to shift.

Would you like to be able to not only recognise, but also quickly shift the way you feel before it escalates?

Welcome to "Rate your State!"

This is something I started after my life collapsed last year. I refused to allow my external circumstances to govern my internal state of mind. I have experienced some very 'dark dips' in the past and the thought of going back there petrified me. I have two children who look up to me, I had no idea if I could be the positive role model I aspired to be but I was going to give it my all to make sure my head didn't end up in a worse mess than my life was.

Step 1: The first step is to make the decision that you want to change. If you remember back to chapter 2 'Find a way or find an excuse' I am hoping that if you have read this far you have found your 'why' and have committed to find a way to make this happen.

Step 2: The second step is to 'Rate your State'. Each day I would check in with myself on a scale of 1-10 and rate how I felt.

I didn't have anything written down or an official chart of what each number equated to but here is an idea of the two extremes.

0 = Today I won't be getting dressed. I will be in bed, the duvet will remain over my head, possibly accompanied by tears streaming down my face and snot streaming from my nose.

10 = Today I will be dressed wearing full make up, hair curled, drinking frothy cappuccinos accompanied by unicorn shaped chocolate sprinkles. I will gallop around my garden on my unicorn, spreading love, light and sparkles to the world!

Ok, so I may have slightly exaggerated my actions of a '10' day (because I don't drink caffeine!) but you get the picture. This a day when you bounce out of bed, everything is going to plan, life feels amazing, and you feel unstoppable.

Based on those two extremes ask yourself, 'What is my number?' There is no right or wrong. I have intentionally not filled in the definitions of the remaining numbers of 1-9 because this number is your perception of how you feel.

Step 3: The third step is to think about one thing you can do to reach just one number higher. That's right, just one number. The problem a lot of people encounter is that when they feel like a 2, they get annoyed and frustrated with themselves and will do one of two things. They either don't take any action so they quickly end up sinking lower to a 1 or a 0, or, they get so annoyed and frustrated that they make a great master plan of how they are going to reach a number 10. I am all for taking responsibility for your feelings but it's not realistic to go from a 2 to a 10 in quick succession. Take the pressure off yourself and ask yourself what is one thing I can do to get myself just one number higher. The amazing power of this is that if you take action and know you can get yourself from a 3 to a 4 then you also have the power to take yourself from a 4 to a 5… and so on.

Here's the secret, don't aim for a 10! Yes, a 10 day is amazing, we all love those days when our superhero cape is flapping behind us, and we feel unstoppable, but it's not realistic to sustain this longer term. For me a 7 is an amazing place to be, but again you decide what feels good for you.

How can you increase your number?

You may be eagerly waiting for my magical solution to climb the 'Rate your State' scale. Here's the thing, I can share with you some of the ways I increase my number but I am me and you are you. I think this is another big mistake we make as humans. If there is a group of people who have the same problem we may wrongly assume that they can all be fixed with the same solution. I say scrap that idea!

You could have a group of 100 women with the same job title, who are all married with children, who are all juggling work and family life and feeling overwhelmed. Each of these women are so unique that it would be very naïve of me to pretend there is a one size fits all solution. Instead, what I can do is tell you how to create your own "Toolbox for Life".

How to create your own "Toolbox for Life"

You are going to add things to your toolbox that make you feel good.

Step 1: Ask yourself how would you like to feel? Happy, calm, relaxed, free, content, peaceful, joyful or hassle-free? (Or all of the above!?)

Step 2: Ask yourself what you can do to create that feeling? (Remember the power of your feelings.) The trick here is the simpler the better, remember the little things are the big things.

Step 3: Make a list of anything and everything that makes you feel happy, calm, relaxed etc and keep adding to your list every time you think of something new. There is no right or wrong here, I will share an extract from my list below. Some may seem a little weird but I'm ok with that. Far too many of us are so busy trying to live life the way we think 'it should be' that we forget to lighten up, have fun, and allow our inner child to be set free. It's ok to be different, you don't always have to follow the crowd. That's enough of my excuses to try and justify my slightly crazy feel-good habits! Here goes:

My feel-good list

Music and Dancing: I listen to songs which make me feel good, turn them up loud and dance. I'm not talking about step together step together boring kind of dancing, I'm talking strut your stuff like no one is watching kind of dancing! I also listen to powerful songs when I need to dig deep for belief and strength in myself.

These are a few of my "feel-good" songs – watch out for the cheese!

What doesn't kill you makes you stronger - Kelly Clarkson

Don't stop me now - Queen

Firework - Katy Perry

You've got the love - The Source featuring Candi Staton

Born this way and *Edge of Glory* - Lady Gaga

Shut up and dance with me - Walk the Moon

Hold my hand - Jess Glynne

Dynamite - Taio Cruz

Firestone - Kygo

Tell it to my heart - Taylor Dayne

Waiting for a star to fall - Boy Meets Girl

These are a few of my "keep going, you can do this songs".

Girl on Fire - Alicia Keyes

Listen - Beyoncé

Hold on - Wilson Phillips

Shine - Take That

Sing - Gary Barlow and the Commonwealth Band Featuring The Military Wives

Fight Song - Rachel Platten

Something inside so strong - Labi Siffre

The world's greatest - R. Kelly

Man in the mirror - Michael Jackson

One moment in time and *Greatest love of all* - Whitney Houston

Read all about it and *Wonder* - Emeli Sandé

Top Tip You can make your own playlist for home or in the car and use the music to help with changing your feelings.

I've just searched online for Emeli Sandé's song, *Read all about it,* to ensure I was spelling her name correctly. I listened to it and have ended up in tears! That wasn't part of the plan, but it just goes to show the power of your feelings. I have a deep emotional connection with many of the songs on my list, and that's ok. I will be sharing some fascinating scientific evidence about tears in chapter 6. You have to let them out; remember supressed emotions aren't good for you. I'm off to get a tissue and then I'll resume my list!

Host your own silent disco: you can take your dancing to another level by plugging in your headphones and having a silent disco (legal disclaimer: not too loud!). It may seem like a small thing to add headphones to the mix but when you are stood up dancing to your favourite music with headphones on, an added superpower is unleashed. A word of warning, however, my 14-year-old son walked into the kitchen recently whilst I was mid-song, shook his head and said, 'Yep, Mum has lost the plot!'.

I have recently found out that The Shard, Western Europe's tallest building, hosts a silent disco every Saturday night – in association with *Time Out London* - on their 69th floor. I would absolutely love to experience this. Maybe I could host my book launch there with a silent disco for all the guests! (Earth to Cassie, earth to Cassie – get your head out of the clouds and get back to writing your feel-good list from your kitchen table in Kettering!)

Calming music: if I feel myself getting worried about something, listening to classical music can quickly calm me down. *Walking through Clouds* by Bernward Koch is an album I love (available from Amazon and all good music shops). I have also recently discovered Taylor Davis, a very talented violinist. Her stunning cover of *Now we are free* has helped me to calm and refocus many, many times. As I write I am listening to *River flows through you* by Yiruma, such a beautiful piece of music. Both of these can be found on YouTube. I often listen to calming music in the car to help me to relax.

Laughing: there is a video on YouTube that I literally cannot watch without laughing, even if I am in a foul mood it makes me laugh out loud Every. Single. Time.

If you want to see if it has the same effect on you search for "Helium beer test, short version with English subtitles" or try this link https://www.youtube.com/watch?v=3V9QHBgrPNY. I've just watched it again, purely for research purposes, and I am now sat here, laughing out loud even though I've seen it so many times. I once shared this video with two random strangers who were behind me in a very busy and crowded card shop a few months ago. We were in a long queue that wasn't going anywhere fast, and the atmosphere was tense and everyone just wanted to pay and escape asap. I can't remember how the conversation started but as we were near a helium balloon machine I guess that may have triggered it. I asked the couple behind me if they had seen the helium beer YouTube video and loaded it on my phone. At this point they may have thought, who on earth is this crazy lady? But within minutes we had gone from stressed out customers in the queue to laughing our heads off! To this day I have no idea who they were, but I do know we all left the shop with smiles on our faces.

Talking: the 24/7 world of 'social' media can, ironically, leave us feeling very disconnected and alone as it can minimise the amount of real-life conversations we have. I make sure I pick up the phone and speak to a friend or arrange to meet up for a cup of tea and a chat so I have something to look forward to.

Eating and drinking: I will cook a good healthy meal and make sure I am drinking lots of water, sometimes I go wild and add a slice of lemon!

Getting dressed: on those really rubbish days my cosy pjs can feel so snug. But I know that even having a shower, using my favourite products, washing my hair and putting on some make-up is enough to make me feel so much better. I always wear my favourite perfume too.

Walking: no matter how rubbish I feel and how unmotivated I am to leave the house, going for a walk always helps. It doesn't matter if it's ten minutes or an hour, it always helps to get some fresh air in my lungs and a fresh perspective on life. I will make eye contact and smile at anyone I pass and if this is reciprocated we will say 'hello' or 'good morning'. Yes, shock, horror I just admitted that I do talk to strangers! Humans crave interaction and just that small act of a smile can make the difference to someone else's day.

Getting outdoors: if it's not possible to go for a walk, just going out into my garden helps me feel better. If it's cold I'll wrap up warm and drink a cup of tea, if it's warm I'll sit, and have a cold drink or sometimes just walk around in bare feet on the grass.

Gardening: that's right. I'm not quite forty yet, but I'm not embarrassed to admit I enjoy gardening. I'm also not embarrassed to admit that I don't have a clue what I'm doing most of the time but I do get a lot of compliments about my garden and take pride in keeping it nice. I have discovered that using a pair of shears can release a lot of stored up anger, too, ha ha!

Reading: I used to think I didn't have time to read, yet somehow, I always found enough time to watch a lot of rubbish on TV! When we moved to a new house last year I made the decision not to have a TV. This was to keep our living costs down as living in a safe area took priority over 60 digital TV channels. I can honestly say I haven't missed it and I have read so many amazing books which have lifted my mood and helped me escape reality.

Writing: as a very calm person, it may surprise some people that I do get angry. I don't like shouting so I choose to express my anger through writing. If I am angry with a person or at a situation I write a letter, but I never send the letter. This may sound like a strange concept but it's very effective way to release emotions that would otherwise get buried.

Having fun: I enjoy simple activities like going to the park, playing on the swings, going down a slide, going on a boat trip, eating ice cream and having a picnic. They all bring back happy memories of being a carefree child. You don't have to have children to take part!

Sleeping: although sleeping can't fix problems or change situations, I know that if I am exhausted and sleep deprived then going to bed at a reasonable time at night or having a power nap in the day can help to recharge my energy.

It's your turn.

What will you include on your feel-good list? It may be something that you used to do but just stopped due to life becoming busy.

Top Tip Write your list down and keep adding to it every time you think of something new.

The majority of the activities on my list are free or cost a very small amount of money. This reiterates my point of the little things being the big things. When you lose so much in your life it can feel like you have very little control, it makes you appreciate the simple things and allows you to find joy. You may have activities that cost more money like going for a swim, joining a yoga class or booking a hair appointment, and that's ok too, it's whatever feels good for you.

From now on start to check in with yourself daily.

Step 1) Ask yourself "What is my number?"

Step 2) Once you know your number pick something to do from your feel-good list.

What you choose is important, but what is even more significant is the **feeling** that the activity brings. Remember how I shared the power of the "F" word? Feelings are the quickest way to increase your number and will help you to climb up the "Rate your State" scale.

When you read through your feel-good list you may be surprised to see that you are already doing some of these, but I'm guessing you only do them when you *feel good*. The secret to staying at a 5 or above is **not** just doing your feel-good list when you're feeling good, do it as often as you can. Check your number daily and if you do slip, it will drastically increase the speed at which you catch yourself falling and this will help you to climb back up quicker. Just knowing you have created your 'Toolkit for Life' gives you a huge sense of reassurance and control.

When I remember back to my 3 day 'dark dip' that I shared in the introduction I felt frustrated as I 'had no reason' to feel down. Nothing big had happened to trigger my mood slipping to a 2, and this made me feel even worse because I didn't know why it had crept up on me so quickly. It was half- term week. I love being able to work from home so I can be there for my children but sometimes this means that it's more challenging to do a lot of the activities from my feel-good list.

I wasn't walking to school and back with my son each day. I wasn't talking as much to adults as I didn't have any work meetings. We had a couple of lazy days, as the boys wanted to chill out. I was also going to bed late as I didn't have to be out early for the school run. What I realised is that when I start on the feeling bad slippery slope, I do the opposite of what's on my feel-good list! It's good to be aware of this so I'm going to share my feel-rubbish list with you too.

My "feel-rubbish" list

*Stay up late so I wake up feeling exhausted.

*Eat more sugary and processed foods.

*Spend hours scrolling through my social media newsfeed.

*Read the newspapers.

*Spend time on my own, don't speak to anyone.

*Avoid going out unless necessary, don't speak to anyone.

*Mope around, feel sorry for myself, don't get dressed.

Can you relate to this?

What do you do when you feel bad that you know makes you feel worse?

Write these down your "feel rubbish list" as reminder of what not to do.

One of the best parts of "Rate your State" is that **you choose** your number, **you choose** your feel-good list and **you choose** the action to increase your state.

On day 3 of my "dark dip" I had been on a work Skype call for over an hour, and in that time my youngest son had broken a chair and was literally climbing the walls. Having previously not wanted to go out I told him that we were going to the park. By the time we had walked there and got a huge ice cream we were both feeling so much better. I then proceeded to dribble chocolate sauce down my white t-shirt and we couldn't stop laughing. I looked like a complete wally walking around the park for the next two hours with a brown stained top but I didn't care. What mattered was that we were having fun. I remember sitting watching him play with some new friends he'd made, feeling the sun on my face and thinking why didn't I go out sooner?! By the time we'd walked home (and I'd binned my top!) we were both in a much better mood.

If you start to look at what has contributed to the chaos of your life you will often find that it is not one big problem that has led you to feeling overwhelmed. It's the little things that have all built up over time, sometimes they are so small you have just accepted them as your normality, but if these are not resolved they can erupt. Have you ever had one of those days when anything and everything gets on your nerves and then one unsuspecting person asks you one innocent question and you literally explode and lose the plot!?

We are all guilty of these cringe-worthy moments. It wasn't the unsuspecting person's fault, it was a build-up of all the little things. There is no escape from the aftermath of awkwardness as you end up apologising for allowing the angry person within you to escape!

These are some things that make me go "Arrrggghh!"

*Drivers who don't acknowledge if I let them out whilst driving.

*Cold callers who don't ask 'is it a good time to talk' before trying to sell me something.

*Football fans discussing a team as if they actually play for them eg "WE didn't win this week but WE have got a good chance in OUR next game".

*People who constantly check their phone whilst in a conversation with you.

*People who practically walk into you as they gaze down at their smart phones.

*Spending 3 hours trying to build a Lego Dimensions portal that keeps on collapsing (Lennie still tells people about how his usually very calm mum nearly threw his favourite birthday present out of the window)!

*Crowded/noisy supermarkets.

*Crowded/noisy coffee shops.

*Busy motorways.

*When my laptop chooses to do an "important update" and restarts when I'm in the middle of a task.

 *The automated voice in the supermarket who tells you there is an unsuspected item in the bagging area and the automated voice on my sat nav who tells me to take a U-turn as soon as possible!

You may well be reading these, rolling your eyes thinking, "Calm down, calm down" (in a Liverpudlian accent). These are only little things so what is the big deal?

Becoming aware of the little things that make you go "Arrrggghh!" allows you to have a greater self-awareness which gives you a better chance of keeping your feelings positive, especially if there are some big things going on in your life - which I will cover in chapter 6.

It's your turn.

What are the little things that make you go "Arrrggghh?!"

Write down your "Things that make you go 'Arrrggghh'" list.

There will always be those which are out of your control. For example I can't control whether the supermarket is going to be busy but I can plan to do my food shop midweek when it's quieter. I have been known to go at 7am to avoid too many people! I will also avoid taking my children to the supermarket.

I can't control how busy the motorway will be but when I have to make a long journey, I prefer to leave as early as possible, even if this means arriving early and stopping in a (hopefully not too busy!) coffee shop.

I can't control the annoying sat nav lady but I can plan my route in advance in the hope that I bypass her U-turn command, and she proceeds to inform me I have arrived at my destination without incident!

Look over your list and see if there are any small changes you can make to ease the burden of these.

What's stopping you?

Life is busy. Be honest, are you using the busyness of life as an excuse not to do the things on your feel-good list? I remember watching a webinar and the lady reminded us that we all have the same 24 hours in the day, and that even if we slept for 8 hours and worked for 8 hours we are still left with 8 hours! Can you find a way to spend 30 minutes a day doing something from your feel-good list?

You are the most important person in your life

We are all extremely good at putting ourselves at the bottom of the pile. Looking after everyone else's needs all the time and then wondering why we feel run down and overwhelmed. That needs to stop right now. How can you look after everyone else if you are constantly exhausted?

Give yourself permission to look after yourself first, if you put yourself at the top of the list everyone else around you will benefit. You will immediately begin to feel calmer, more confident and back in control. This will ripple into every area in your life.

Nothing in this chapter is rocket science, there is no miraculous overnight solution but now you have your

"Toolbox for Life" you can take a big step in the right direction and get back into the driver's seat of your life.

Rule 4: The little things are the big things.

You can reduce the severity and length of your dark dips by using the "Rate your State" game. Check in daily to see how you are feeling and use your own "Toolbox for Life" so that you can quickly recognise and change your negative thoughts into positive feelings.

Make the activities on your feel-good list a priority, not just when you feel good.

Have an awareness of the little things in your life which make you go "Arrrggghh" so that these can be managed, where possible, to reduce stress levels.

Never underestimate the power of what really matters in your life, the little things.

Rule 5 - Embrace the power of the "M" word!

Do you remember the character Violet Beauregarde in the film *Charlie and the Chocolate Factory*? For those of you who haven't watched it, Violet is an impatient and impulsive child who is known for her demanding outbursts of, "I want it NOW!" Violet is a fictional character in a children's film but if we're honest there is a little bit of Violet in all of us.

We live in a world where we can have pretty much anything we want 24/7 at the touch of a button. Back in my day (my goodness, don't I sound old?) I remember when kids' TV programmes were only on after 4pm and on a Saturday morning, and if you wanted to watch a film you had to hire a video from the local video shop. The high street shops were only open 9am- 5pm.

We now have 24-hour supermarkets and gyms and if we want to buy anything we don't have to save, we have access to credit cards and interest free deals! Although we are very fortunate, we are also a bit spoilt. I'm not implying that we all go around shouting, "I want it NOW!" but actually we don't want to wait for anything. If something takes too much time or effort we give up, and quickly follow up with an excuse to justify our lack of patience.

Your new "Toolbox for Life" might seem all new, fresh and exciting now and may have filled you with hope for living in a way where you are feeling calmer and back in control, and rightfully so. As I said, they are very powerful tools, but only if you are consistently using them on a regular basis. Let's go back to the example I gave in chapter 2 of wanting to get fit and lose weight.

It can take 4 weeks of making healthy choices and regular exercise before you see a difference in your body.

It can take up to 8 weeks of making healthy choices and regular exercise before other people notice a difference.

NB: this is not a scientific fact, it is from a meme on Pinterest!

The reason for sharing this example is that in the grand scheme of things, 4 or 8 weeks is not a long period of time. However, when you are trying to plan your meals, buy the right foods, avoid all temptation, and cut down on alcohol it can feel like forever!

It can be easy to fall off the health kick wagon and back into your old ways, which is why so many people yoyo diet for years and lose track of how many times they have given up and started again - on a Monday, of course!

You can be faced with similar challenges when you are trying to decrease your stress levels and take back the control in your head. As I mentioned in chapter 1, you are trying to undo years and years of negative thoughts, layers and old habits. If you start to use your "Toolbox for Life" consistently I believe you will notice a positive change after 4 weeks and those around you will notice after 8 weeks, maybe even sooner. But with the daily pressures and challenges from your life this may feel like forever away.

Do you want results NOW?

The secret ingredient for faster results is the "M" word.

You know, the "M" word that you will either love or hate.

Was your first guess Marmite? I love marmite, like *really* love it! Every single packed lunch I ever took to school as a child contained 3 marmite rolls every single day. Anyway, enough of my compulsive Marmite eating - the "M" word that I want to talk to you about is MEDITATION.

Did you just roll your eyes? Haha, that's ok, I also used to roll my eyes at the "M" word. As with the "F" word all I ask is that you read on with an open mind, and if at the end of this chapter, the "M" word is still not for you then that is completely fine. I won't be dragging anyone kicking and screaming onto the woo woo bus! I debated (with myself!) whether to include this chapter and the conclusion that I came to (by myself!) is that it would be very unfair of me not to share this.

Let's start by getting this out on the open.

Why you may dislike meditation:

1) You are fed up of being asked to count backwards from 100 as you sit under your special tree, feel the wind in your hair and balance your root chakra!
2) You may get bored and impatient listening to the really looooooong and boring introduction and being told how to breathe whilst sitting up straight with your legs crossed.
3) You feel frustrated when you are told to conjure up a completely unrealistic made-up scenario. Instead of feeling relaxed you may feel like screaming, "This is not real life!"
4) The stranger whose voice is meant to be calming you down is actually irritating you as they speak in a very monotone, very serious and very stern voice. Surely, they don't really speak like that!?
5) The music that accompanies the stranger's voice is boring and dull, or worse still there is no music.
6) The length of the overall meditation is far too long. If you do manage to make it to the end (calmly

sealing yourself in a bubble of golden light!) you don't actually feel any different to when you started. Well, maybe irritated that you've just wasted half an hour!

Ways you might be persuaded to love meditation:

Research* shows that meditation:

1) Increases positive emotions.
2) Increases life satisfaction.
3) Boots your immune function.
4) Decreases pain.
5) Decreases inflammation.
6) Increases memory.
7) Improves attention.
8) Increases social connection.
9) Reduces loneliness.
10) Increases cortical thickness in your brain, especially in areas related to introspection and attention.
11) Increases grey matter in areas related to memory (hippocampus) and thought (frontal areas).
12) Increases brain volume specifically in areas for emotion regulation, positive emotions and self-control.
13) Decreases anxiety.
14) Decreases stress.
15) Decreases depression.

*This is a summary of an article in *Psychology Today*, written by Emma Seppälä PhD, on '20 Science-based reasons to start meditating today' where you can find the direct sources quoted.

www.emmaseppala.com/20-scientific-reasons-to-start-meditating-today.

That's an impressive list, right? But is it possible to stop banging your head on the metaphorical woo woo wall and bring some real-life meditation into your life that actually works?

Absolutely!

How can you put an end to your love/hate relationship with meditation?

I want to take you back to the summer of 2012 when my life had collapsed for the second time. I had dragged myself along to a mindset training day in the hope of rediscovering some of the pieces of my motivation (which had been missing in action for far too long).

That day I met a man who helped me to change my life, Dave O'Connor. As I sat in the audience I was glued to his every word, I wasn't in a very good place in my head but everything Dave said made so much sense. All of a sudden I found a glimmer of hope that I could turn my life around. As soon as Dave spoke about working together on a one to one basis I knew I had to invest in myself and he was the man who was going to help me. It was one of those moments when I couldn't afford to work with Dave, but I also couldn't afford not to work with him. I remember on our first call I said to him, "No pressure, Dave, but this is make or break."

We would have a coaching call and then Dave would make me a personalised meditation (a blueprint as he called it). Until this time, I had never found a meditation that I had liked, let alone listened to more than once. His meditations were so powerful that I would often cry listening to them - happy tears by the way. It was the combination of hearing my personal goals and how I wanted to feel, along with a familiar voice that I trusted and the beautiful background music that led to a very powerful transformation. This was at a time in my life when I could have easily given up on everything.

It was working with Dave that gave me a very powerful insight. The first time my life collapsed I was in a complete mess and I self- destructed. The second time my life collapsed I could have been a much bigger mess but I realised that despite all the external chaos, my mind was extremely calm and piece by piece I managed to rebuild my life. I know that without a shadow of a doubt listening daily to these personal meditations that Dave made for me played a huge part in this.

Fast forward 6 months, and against all the odds I had set up my own business making bespoke meditations for women to help restore their body confidence. I will never forget the first one I made, sat in my kitchen nervously recording on a Dictaphone whilst playing the background music on my laptop! Some of my friends were personal trainers who kindly allowed me to work with their clients so that I could receive some testimonials. The amazing results of my work shocked the trainers and the clients – but no one was more surprised than I was when the testimonials came in a few weeks later!

What had I done?

I was inspired to scrap the traditional meditation rules and committed to making real meditations for real transformations.

1) There is no counting backwards, wind blowing in your hair or balancing of chakras. If fact there is no woo woo to be seen (or heard!) Personally, I love a bit of woo woo, so much so that I have recently become a Reiki Master, but I like my meditations to be real.

2) The introduction is never any longer than 10 seconds and will never insist you sit up straight with your hands on your lap or sit crossed legged. The majority of the time I meditate I am curled up on my sofa with a cosy blanket over me.

3) I have a one-hour Skype call with my client to establish exactly what it is they are hoping to achieve and how they want to feel.
4) I use their name in the meditation – this is extremely powerful.
5) Having searched for three days, I record my meditations with the most beautiful, calming and uplifting music I could find.
6) Each meditation never lasts for any longer than five minutes.

Over the last 4 years I have developed the ability to create a range of meditations which can be tailor made for any work or life situations where you want to increase your confidence and feel calmer.

You'll be pleased to know I binned the Dictaphone and now use more sophisticated recording software! We all have to start somewhere, don't we?

But it doesn't make sense!

Can years and years of negativity, layers and bad habits be undone by listening to a five-minute meditation each day? That's not logical, is it?

Remember the power of "F" word?

The reason my meditations can be so powerful in just minutes is that they connect on a deep emotional level.

This is where the power of feelings come into their own. It's actually not the meditation that brings this new perceived superpower, it's the **feelings** that the meditation creates and leaves you with.

Consistent (eg once a day) meditation will help you to feel better faster, and quickly increase your 'Rate your State' number by creating feelings that are fuelled by your very own inner rocket-power!

The science bit

This is another extract from Chris Walton's book.

"Psychologists identify two separate minds: the conscious mind and the subconscious mind. Your conscious mind is the thinking part that is associated with your personal identity. It is involved in logic, reasoning and decision making.

Your 'other' mind is the subconscious which is generally known to be the place of your programmed and learned actions, responses and behaviours. All of the involuntary systems of the body are run by the subconscious mind. For example, your heart beats approximately 100,000 times a day, sending over 100 gallons of blood through your vascular system, yet you don't have to consciously tell it to do so or direct its action. The majority of your mental and emotional reactions are also processed at a subconscious level.

The power of your subconscious mind

The conscious and subconscious minds can be likened to information processors each being able to process a certain amount of energy and information. Think of each as having a certain bandwidth of processing power that can be measured in bits per second (bps). Staggeringly, the processing power of the subconscious mind is a whopping 400,000,000 bits of information per second.

Now compare that with the conscious mind which can process a mere 40 bits of information per second. **The subconscious mind has one million times more processing power than the conscious mind.**

Aligning your subconscious mind with your conscious goals dramatically increases your ability to manifest your goals."

From *The Gamma Mindset* by Chris Walton MSc
www.GammaMindset.com

Back to non-scientific Cassie

Pretty impressive, isn't it?

Meditation acts as a way to bypass your conscious mind, allowing direct communication with your subconscious mind.

"When you achieve a state of meditation, you unlock the door to your subconscious mind. That is where your power to create the life you deserve lives." Adrian Calbrese

Are you coming on board?

I promised not to drag you kicking and screaming onto the woo woo bus and I am a woman of my word. However, if you would like to climb aboard the bus of your own accord then let me welcome you.

If you would like to download a complimentary meditation I have made for you to experience this power for yourself you can head to www.cassiefarren.com

Remember, consistency is key! Going back to my first example of losing weight, you wouldn't expect to lose weight by eating one salad each month, so meditating once a month also won't make a difference.

Top Tips for Meditation

*Set an alarm on your phone to remind yourself to listen at least once a day.

*For best results listen once a day either first thing in the morning or last thing at night.

*Wear headphones when you listen – no scientific proof here - but it definitely makes it feel more powerful.

*If you feel like you are going down the "Rate your State" scale you would benefit from listening more than once a day.

*Never listen to a meditation when driving or operating machinery.

There are 1440 minutes in a day, so there's no excuse if you can't take 5 minutes out for a meditation.

Rule 5: Embrace the power of the "M" word.

Meditation acts as a way to bypass your conscious mind, allowing direct communication with your subconscious mind. It will speed up your results to living a calmer life and it will also get you back on track if you fall off the wagon at any point.

You can download your complimentary relaxation MP3 from www.cassiefarren.com

Commit to listening once a day to feel calmer and back in control.

You are now equipped with your "Toolbox for Life" as well as an extra superpower (aka meditation) so you are well on your way to feeling calmer and in control of your life. But what happens when the unexpected hits the fan?

Find out in the next chapter!

Rule 6 - It's okay not to be okay

There will always be times in life when the big things dominate the little things. We've all had those times when life dumps a great big pile of chaos on our doorstep and like it or not, ready or not, we have to deal with it. Sometimes this is expected chaos, other times it's a bolt from the blue. Both can be incredibly challenging, especially if we are trying our hardest to carry on living a normal life.

As frustration kicks in, there is a tendency to try and fix things or make it all better as quickly as possible. Sadly, I am yet to discover a magic wand for the 'Rate your State' 0 days when you just want to go back to bed, hide under your duvet and reappear when you're feeling a little braver.

But while there's no magic wand, there is an alternative, and I'm going to share with you what has helped me emerge from the duvet and pick myself up when it's all hit the fan.

It's okay not to be okay

When your world crumbles around you it can be devastating. What makes the devastation worse is feeling out of control. You may initially feel angry, upset, scared, alone, frustrated, or a combination of all of these. As I mentioned in The "F" word chapter, we are conditioned to believe that emotions are a sign of weakness. Were you ever told to "stop crying like a baby" when you were growing up? Or that you should "pull yourself together" if you showed a perceived emotion?

I have also done a lot of "pretending to be okay" over the years and I've come to the conclusion that the only person you are hurting is yourself. Your bottled-up emotions will come out sooner or later. You can only pretend to be okay for so long. What I do now is give myself permission to feel and express my emotions, and you might find this works for you too. If you want to cry, cry. If you want to sob and wail, sob and wail. Allowing your emotions to come out may not feel great at the time but if that's what needs to come out then let it come out.

I found an interesting blog written by Judith Orloff MD in *Psychology Today* which shares the benefits of our tears.

"Our bodies produce three kinds of tears: reflex, continuous and emotional. Each kind has different healing roles. For instance, reflex tears allow your eyes to clear out noxious particles when they're irritated by smoke or exhaust. The second kind, continuous tears, are produced regularly to keep our eyes lubricated – these contain a chemical called 'lysozyme' which functions as an antibacterial and protects our eyes from infection.

Tears also travel to the nose through the tear duct to keep the nose moist and bacteria free. Typically, after crying, our breathing, and heart rate decrease, and we enter into a calmer biological and emotional state.

Emotional tears have special health benefits. Biochemist and 'tear expert' Dr William Frey at the Ramsey Medical Center in Minneapolis discovered that reflex tears are 98% water, whereas emotional tears also contain stress hormones which get excreted from the body through crying. After studying the composition of tears Dr Frey found that emotional tears shed these hormones and other hormones and other toxins which accumulate during stress. Additional studies also suggest that crying stimulates the production of endorphin, our body's natural pain killer and 'feel-good' hormones."

You've heard it from the experts and you've heard it from me, there is no need to feel ashamed or embarrassed for crying. It is actually good for you.

This morning when I was at my friend Michelle's house, I was telling her about something that had happened at the weekend and as I was speaking I welled up with tears. It wasn't a full-on sobbing and snot moment but it did take me by surprise. A few years ago I would have quickly changed the subject and fought the tears but today I just let them out. Michelle gave me a tissue and a hug and 5 minutes later we were back to chatting and laughing again.

You are not a burden

When I had my emotional moment this morning, Michelle didn't say get out of my house you are a weak mess of a woman. She was genuinely kind, caring and supportive. So why is it that when we get upset we feel like we are a burden to other people? Can you remember a time when a friend or family member has cried or needed your help? If you are a decent human being, which I'm sure you are, you feel an urge to help the person who is upset.

It's okay to accept help

Why is it that we find it so hard to accept help? We will do anything and everything to keep going and find a way to be strong and independent, even in a crisis. In the past I have been guilty of being in the 'I don't need anything' gang. I have now learnt that there are times when you need to swallow your pride and accept help.

It's okay to ask for help

You may have had to read that last sub-header twice. Did you think, oh my goodness did she just write **ask** for help!? Yes, I did and I mean it. As children we ask for help all the time and think nothing of it, yet we enter adulthood and the "H" word disappears from our vocabulary. Once again I used to be guilty of this. I should be able to cope with the beautiful mess of my life just fine, so there is no way I will ask for help. After all, isn't this a sign of weakness?

Last year I found myself in a position where I needed to get out of my own way and start using the "H" word. I swallowed a lot of pride and asked for help. I didn't just ask for help from anyone, I asked my ex-husband! Looking back, perhaps I should have warned him to sit down first before I sent my text. Anyone would be shocked to receive a text from their normally extremely independent ex-wife who began her message with, "I need your help..." Fortunately, he did help, and I will always be grateful for this.

A few months later I found myself in another predicament. I had missed the last train back from London on a Saturday night and went into panic mode. I frantically started texting my friend and asked her to look up hotels and taxis for me, while I tried to get in touch with another friend who lived in London. All the hotels were booked or charging £300. I could not think of any other option but to sleep at St Pancras station or Luton airport, as that was the closest I could get to home. I told myself this was a safer option as there would be security and people around. My friend tried not to laugh at the normally very organised Cassie who was potentially going to be sleeping on a cold airport chair! She said, "Cassie, who can help you? Surely there is someone who could pick you up from Luton?" The first person I thought of was my Dad but cringed at the thought of trying to explain myself and tell him I was really stuck! I started to compose a text but as I was on the train to Luton with little signal and a bunch of loud, drunk football fans who were adding to my increasing stress levels due to a) being loud and lairy and b) shouting about how "WE" won our match today, it took some time and concentration!

I took a deep breath and sent the text asking if there was any way he could drive to collect me from Luton and that I would be eternally grateful. I can't tell you how hard it was to press the "send" button, but within minutes my dad replied, telling me not to worry and that he and my mum would set off on the 45-minute journey from their house straightaway. He also told me to wait inside the station and stay safe. I didn't know whether to laugh or cry with relief knowing that I was going to be rescued by my parents and that I could now sleep soundly in a bed instead of a cold chair at the airport! What a wally! I still can't believe I didn't check the train times home, I had wrongly assumed they would run until the early hours of the morning.

When I got to Luton station I realised that my train ticket had expired in London St Pancras and that I would need to pay an excess charge. I smiled at the man on the ticket barrier and explained I had made a genuine mistake and was happy to pay and could I wait in the station until I was rescued by my parents!? I swear the man was an angel in disguise. He was very understanding, didn't charge me and chatted to me until my parents arrived. He even offered my parents a drink on arrival as he knew they had driven a long way! You may have giggled at this story and that's ok, believe me, I have since laughed too. But in all seriousness, I've shared it to show that no matter how organised or in control you are in your life the unexpected can still happen. If you ask for help, people are normally extremely willing to help you.

Since that episode, I have had several people tell me if it ever happens again (which it won't as I now always make sure I check the return train times!) to give them a ring. They would have hated the thought of me sleeping at the airport just because I was too proud to ask for help.

If I can be brave and ask for help then you can too. I used to feel like if someone helped me that I should immediately do something to help them back. I now remind myself that I help a lot of people, you don't always have to help the same person you can pay it forward and help someone else - which brings me onto my next point.

Who can you help?

This may seem like a strange concept if you are going through a challenging time yourself but the act of helping others can be extremely rewarding. This can be something as small as holding the door open for someone, letting another driver out or allowing someone to go in front of you in a queue.

On Christmas Day and Boxing Day in 2012, I volunteered at a homeless centre in central London run by Crisis. Many people thought I had officially lost the plot and wondered why I hadn't spent Christmas Day with my children, but we had our Christmas Day on Christmas Eve instead. Having ended my marriage earlier in the year I was dreading the thought of having half a day with my children, and the other half of the day ~~drinking wine and feeling sorry for myself whilst watching Bridget Jones~~ on my own. This is what happened instead.

I woke up early on Christmas Day; the house was too quiet. I kept thinking of the boys, but just reminded myself we had already had our Christmas Day. I have no idea what possessed me to log onto my Facebook account before I began my drive into central London. My newsfeed on a normal day can get on my nerves with the sometimes exaggerated "Everything is so perfect in my life" posts. As expected, they were everywhere that morning. People couldn't wait to share "My children have opened their huge mountain of presents", "I can't wait to see my amazing family", "This is the best Christmas ever" – and it was only 7am! I am aware I may sound like a complete Scrooge but when you have spent Christmas Day without your close family and your children, it does make you spare a thought for others who are alone or missing family members.

It can be an extremely difficult day and a very sad time of the year. One Facebook post which caught my eye certainly wasn't a happy one. A guy who was volunteering at the same homeless centre was devastated that his motorbike had broken down near Luton. He was really upset and apologising that for the first time in years he wasn't going to make it to volunteer, as there was no public transport available. I thought how upset I would be if my car had broken down that morning; it's not like you can tag along to someone else's Christmas Day, is it? Having to sit on your own all day with no plans would be awful.

Without thinking twice, I replied to his post saying I would be passing Luton in an hour and would be happy to pick him up! I'm not stupid, I know it's not in the "Health and Safety" etiquette to drive to a random guy's house and drive them into central London! But sometimes you have to trust your instincts. It was Christmas Day and I wanted to help. I pulled up in his street and called him to say I was the girl outside in the silver car, as I realised we didn't know what each other looked like! We chatted and laughed all the way into London and, as he had volunteered before, he knew exactly where to go and exactly where to park, which was a huge relief.

When we walked in, I suddenly felt apprehensive. It was meant to be a happy day but I was conscious of how all the homeless people would be feeling. Could I hold it together and keep a lid on my emotions? I had no idea what to expect as I made my way to register and was shown to the room where I would be working. I will never forget my time there; it was an experience that is so difficult to put into words. There were hundreds of volunteers, all working together as a big team, which created an amazing atmosphere. It was the most humbling experience I've ever had. My life was far from perfect but it reminded me to be grateful for what I had.

Flip your thoughts

This is something that I started doing a few years ago to try and keep calm and I still do it now. If you have a negative thought try and flip it around into something positive.

Negative – I hate going food shopping.

Positive – I have enough money for food.

Negative – I hate washing up every night.

Positive – I am washing up as I've eaten food.

Negative – I'm stuck in a traffic jam on the way to a meeting.

Positive – I have a car and I also have a job/business.

Negative – I am running around like a mad woman getting ready for the school run.

Positive – I am taking my child/children to school.

It may seem like a small thing to do, and it doesn't change the task in hand but the more you train your brain to see the positive the more you will automatically begin to recognise the positive.

Friends will be friends

When a big life challenge gets thrown at you there may be people who disappear into thin air and others who want to speak to you more than usual. It's important to talk but remember that you are in charge of who you speak to. Don't feel you have to explain everything to everyone all the time. It is draining and you need all of your energy for you.

Social media

I would avoid updating your status with cryptic messages such as 'Cassie is feeling upset/angry/frustrated' as this can trigger a rush of online 'friends' wanting to know more. A small group of friends who you can speak to in real life or on the phone is much more supportive. It's ok for you to say, "Do you mind if we don't talk about this today as I'm feeling really drained" if you don't want to talk.

I decided to delete all social media apps (as well as my e-mail) from my phone a few months ago and it was one of the best things I've done. It felt a bit strange a first but it had become too easy to pop on quickly only to find myself wasting time watching a random cat video! I now log on a few times a day (mainly Monday-Friday) from my laptop which has freed up so much space in my head. Is this something that may benefit you? I told my close friends that if they needed me to call or to go back to good old-fashioned text as I no longer had access to messages through social media.

Do you find your phone is constantly beeping with notifications even when you leave your house? You may choose to turn off your wi-fi or mobile data. Making these small changes has helped me so much that I am now in control on my phone, instead of the other way around.

The mini to-do list

It can feel overwhelming to have a huge long list of things to do, so instead, try making a master list of everything that needs to be actioned and choose 3 items per day. Once these have been completed you can choose 3 more to do and so on.

Look after yourself

It can be tempting to try doing everything on your "feel rubbish list" when you feel rubbish but longer term this isn't going to help. Going back to the basics of eating well, drinking less caffeine and alcohol and getting plenty of rest will make the world of difference. Go back your "Toolbox for Life" even if you can do one activity a day it can help to get you through the harder times.

What can you look forward to?

This could be going out for lunch with a friend, a massage at a spa or a daytrip to the seaside - anything that helps to focus on moving forward.

It's not always easy but keep on taking one day at a time and don't look too far ahead, you are stronger than you know.

Remember that your track record of getting through bad days is pretty good, you have got through every single one and you are still here now.

If you have followed the guidance so far in my book combined with your new "Toolbox for Life" you will have now found a powerful way to release the unnecessary stress from your head which will enable you to take back your control and move forward to living a calmer life, even when the unexpected hits the fan.

Top Tip Remember to check out my 'Resources' page if you need any additional support and always speak to a health professional if you feel you need urgent advice or help.

Rule 6: It's okay not to be okay.

When life throws a big challenge at you it's okay to ask for help and it's okay to accept help.

You are not a burden, it is not a weakness to express your emotions or to cry.

Take one day at a time and always remember to look after yourself.

Does following "The Rules" mean that your life will be stress-free from now on?

All will be revealed in the next chapter.

Rule 7 - Don't stop now!

The challenge with any self-help book is this. **Self** comes before **help**. No matter how enthusiastic you are when you read the first word on the first page, no matter how many "ah ha" moments you have had through the chapters, when you read the last word on the last page from that moment on it's over to you.

The advantage of my book is that once you begin to take back your control and live by "The Rules" you will be on your way to stress-free living.

Is there such thing as a Stress-Free Life?

I don't believe there is. We all love a 7, 8 or even a 9 "Rate your State" day but it is unrealistic to think that this is sustainable, as let's face it life goes on and life can bring us expected and unexpected challenges along the way. This isn't meant to sound negative, if anything I think it is empowering not to have such high expectations as a lot of our day to day stress is caused by our reality not matching our high expectations of how life should be.

For me stress-free living is the next best thing. When you live by "The Rules" you can learn to let go of the unnecessary stress in your life which *can* you control. If there is a situation which you *can't* control then you can use "The Rules" to free up some space in your head to change your perspective and your feelings associated with the situation.

It's not easy.

These were the first, poignant, words that I wrote in in this book just 8 weeks ago.

One of the biggest misconceptions people can have when they meet me is assuming that I have always been so full of positivity. When I was talking to a lady last week I shared that once my book is published I would love to develop a training programme that can be delivered online or in person to compliment the book. I told her that longer term I would love to licence my programme so that other trainers can also deliver the programme with the intention that it can reach as many people as possible. She said to me, "I love your determination and your belief that you can really make a difference to the world!" I smiled and said, "One person at a time, why not?"

I am fully aware this is a very big vision that, if I'm honest, does slightly scare me at the enormity of it but at the same time as I am writing this book I ask myself the question, why not me, why not now?

If I knew how challenging it was going to be running a business as a single parent I don't think I would have started for the main reason that I wouldn't have thought I had enough strength within me to get through the many challenges that have been thrown in my way.

I am often asked why I haven't quit. How am I still so positive?

The simple answer is that I live by "The Rules".

1) I have given myself a break and stopped emotionally beating myself up about the perceived mistakes I have made in my past. I took control of the negative voice in my head and know that I have done the best I can with the resources I've had. I knew that before I changed my life I had to change the way I thought.

2) I have a very strong "why" to be a positive role model to my children. I want to show them that no matter what happens in their life they always have a choice and that you are not defined by your circumstances. I also want to inspire others that they too can let go of their past and take back the control of their future. I have committed to finding a way to do this, no matter what. Excuses, victim mode and P.O.M syndrome have been evicted from my life.

3) I embrace the "F" word in all areas of my life. I understand the power of feelings and always acknowledge, honour and express them.

4) I know that the little things are the big things. I have created my "Toolbox for Life" and regularly "Rate my State" so that I can quickly shift the way I feel. I make my emotional and physical wellbeing a priority without feeling any guilt and I know how to pick myself up quickly if I feel a "dark dip" coming on.

5) The "M"' word has become a non-negotiable part of my life. I understand the proven benefits and I listen to a meditation at least once a day, knowing that this is the quickest way to reach a higher number if I start to slide down the "Rate your State" scale.

6) I understand that it is not a weakness to ask for help. If I need help I ask for it, if help is offered to me I accept it, if there is a way that I can offer help to someone else I will.

7) I don't just talk and write about "The Rules" I make sure that I am implementing and including them in all areas of my life, all the time. I take full responsibility for making "The Rules" a priority in my life as there is no one else in my life who can change my life apart from me.

I am living proof that if I can live by "The Rules" then you can too.

"The Rules" - A Summary

Rule 1: Give yourself a break.

You now know that the overwhelm in your head is not your fault. It has built up due to an accumulation of 'life layers' which have built up over many years. These layers have joined forces with the added pressure of work, family and financial pressure with extra added pressure from social media and the busyness of everyday life.

Draw a line under what has been and gone. Your past can't be changed, but from now on you can commit to living a calmer life where you are in control. Make the decision to stop emotionally beating yourself up and decide that you are ready to incorporate stress-free living into your life.

Rule 2: Find a way or find an excuse.

Creating a positive lasting change in your life begins with finding your 'why'.

You know the importance of letting go of your old excuses and P.O.M syndrome. Finding your 'why' will help you to keep your motivation, even when challenges occur.

Excuses are just words that you use to justify not being responsible. If you give away the power of your responsibility then you are not in control. If you are not in control you will never be able to make a positive lasting change in your head or your life.

Rule 3: Embrace the power of the "F" word!

We are creatures of habit and it's not easy to change, but when you can engage your heart and connect your feelings to your goals, that is where the power is.

You know that your feelings have the power to override your negative thoughts. They can literally help you to take back the control in your head and ultimately your life.

Rule 4: The little things are the big things!

"Rate Your State" has taught you how to recognise and recover quicker from a "dark dip". It can also help you to keep your feelings positive which can help to counteract those negative thoughts.

You know that making the activities on your feel-good list should be a priority all of the time, not just when you feel good.

You have an awareness of the little things in your life which make you go "Arrrggghh" so that these can be managed, where possible, to reduce stress levels.

Never underestimate the power of what really matters in your life, the little things.

Rule 5: Embrace the power of the "M" word!

You know that meditation is scientifically proven to have multiple benefits which includes decreasing stress, anxiety and increases positive emotions. It will speed up your results to living a calmer life and it will also get you back on track if you fall off the wagon at any point.

Meditation acts as a way to bypass your conscious mind, allowing direct communication with your subconscious mind.

You can download your complimentary relaxation MP3 from www.cassiefarren.com

Commit to listening to your meditation once a day to feel calmer and back in control.

Rule 6: It's okay not to be okay.

You know that if life throws a big challenge at you it's okay to take off your Superhero cape.

It's okay to ask for help and it's okay to accept help.

You are not a burden. It is not a weakness to express your emotions or to cry.

Take one day at a time and always remember to look after yourself.

Rule 7: Don't stop now!

You know that it is your responsibility to implement these new tools and techniques so that you can take back your control and live a calmer life.

You know that to make a difference you have to be consistent and make a commitment to yourself that from now on you will live by your new rules!

You now know how to

Reduce Your Stress, Regain Your Control & Restore Your Calm so that you too can

Rule Your World.

Cassie

P.S Remember to connect with me on Twitter @cassiefarren1 and share your favourite rule using #RuleYourWorld

P.P.S Come and connect with me in the FREE "Rule Your World" Facebook group for support and inspiration. www.facebook.com/groups/ruleyourworldtribe

Resources

Action for Happiness: www.actionforhappiness.org

British Association for Counselling & Psychotherapy: www.bacp.co.uk

Heads Together: www.headstogether.org.uk

Live Happy: www.livehappy.com

Louise Hay: www.louisehay.com

Mind: www.mind.org.uk

Mindvalley: www.mindvalleyacademy.com

Time to Change: www.time-to-change.org.uk

About the Author

Cassie, who lives in Northamptonshire, England, has been described as "a gentle soul powered by rocket fuel!". Her priority has always been the happiness and security of her family, and she cherishes the moments and the memories they make in the quality time they spend together.

Cassie loves being around the special people in her life, relaxing in the countryside, and exploring new places. Having turned her own life around, Cassie now takes great pride in inspiring others to live the life they know they deserve.

Contact Cassie

To find out more about Cassie and her work, please visit:

www.cassiefarren.com

You can connect with Cassie on social media

Twitter @cassiefarren1 - remember to use #RuleYourWorld

Facebook /cassie.farren

LinkedIn /cassiefarren

For corporate enquiries and professional speaker bookings please e-mail

enquiries@cassiefarren.com

For media enquiries please e-mail

media@cassiefarren.com

Cassie would love you to leave a review for her book on Amazon.

Cassie's First Book

The Girl Who Refused to Quit

*The Girl Who Refused to Qui*t tells the surprisingly uplifting journey of a young woman who has overcome more than her fair share of challenges.

When she hit rock bottom for the third time Cassie was left questioning her worth and her purpose. She could have been forgiven for giving up on everything. Instead she chose to transform adversity into triumph and with not much more than sheer determination Cassie has now set up her own business to empower other women.

She is the girl who refused to be defined by her circumstances. She is the girl who wants to inspire other women, to show them that no matter what challenges you face you can still hold your head high, believe in yourself and follow your dreams.

She is The Girl Who Refused to Quit.

Available on Paperback & Kindle from Amazon
http://amzn.to/2uo4to5